The Graphic Novel

Red Riding Hood

retold by *Martin Powell*
illustrated by *Victor Rivas*

Raintree

www.raintreepublishers.co.uk
Visit our website to find out
more information about
Raintree books.

To order:
☎ Phone 0845 6044371
🖨 Fax +44 (0) 1865 312263
✉ Email myorders@raintreepublishers.co.uk

Customers from outside the UK please telephone +44 1865 312262

Raintree is an imprint of Capstone Global Library Limited, a company incorporated in
England and Wales having its registered office at 7 Pilgrim Street, London EC4V 6LB
Registered company number: 6695882

Text © Stone Arch Books 2009
First published by Stone Arch Books in 2009
First published in paperback in the United Kingdom by Capstone Global Library in 2013
The moral rights of the proprietor have been asserted.

Editor: Laura Knowles
Art Director: Heather Kindseth
Graphic Designer: Kay Fraser
Librarian Reviewer: Katharine Kan
Reading Consultant: Elizabeth Stedem
Printed and bound in China by CTPS

ISBN 978 1 406 24772 5 (paperback)
16 15 14 13 12
10 9 8 7 6 5 4 3 2 1

British Library Cataloguing in Publication Data
Powell, Martin.
Red Riding Hood. -- (Graphic spin)
741.5-dc23
A full catalogue record for this book is available from the British Library.

The Graphic Novel

Red Riding Hood

CAST of CHARACTERS

Grandma

Father

Ruby

Mother

The Wolf

Transylvania.

The Land of Phantoms and the birthplace of almost every scary story ever told.

Come, dear. My crystal ball can tell you much more.

Mercy on you!

What's wrong, Magda? What did you see?

Evil creatures prowl the woods.

They cannot enter our homes unless they are invited inside.

Take this red cloth.

Whatever you make with it will protect you, but only during the daylight hours.

I'm afraid I don't have any money.

16

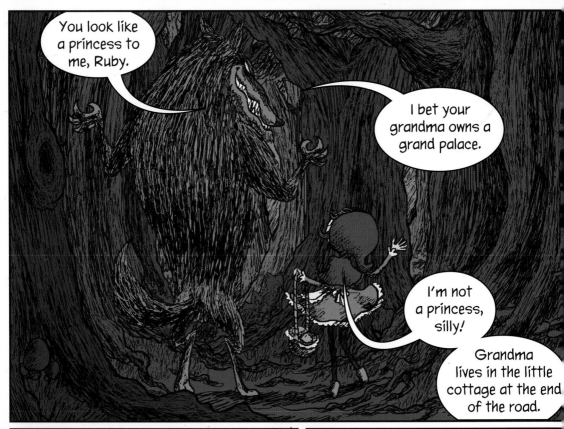

You look like a princess to me, Ruby.

I bet your grandma owns a grand palace.

I'm not a princess, silly!

Grandma lives in the little cottage at the end of the road.

Ah, yes. I know the place you mean.

Grandma hasn't been feeling well, so I'm bringing her some cake and cookies.

I wish I could do something nice for your grandma, too.

Moments later, at Grandma's house . . .

KNOCK!!
KNOCK!!
KNOCK!!

Come on in, child. Just lift the latch.

Meanwhile, back at the clover field . . .

Finally! I found one!

A four-leaf clover!

I didn't think it would take me so long. It'll be dark soon.

I better hurry, so Grandma doesn't worry!

23

See? Here's a whole basket full of goodies and wildflowers for you!

How sweet, my dear.

Grandma's not wearing her glasses. Bring the basket closer, so I can see everything better.

That's not all! A lucky four-leaf clover, just for you!

Now you'll get better for sure!

Oh, how lovely!

Grandma's so weak. Come closer, girl.

25

After that day, Red Riding Hood continued to visit her grandma's cottage often, planting flowers, bringing cookies, and reading her books by the fireplace.

It was her favourite place to be . . .

. . . because her grandma loved the brave girl so very much.

All About Vampires & Werewolves

In fact, more than anything.

About the author

Since 1986, Martin Powell has been a freelance writer. He has written hundreds of stories, many of which have been published by Disney, Marvel, Tekno Comix, Moonstone Books, and others. In 1989, Powell received an Eisner Award nomination for his graphic novel *Scarlet in Gaslight*. This award is one of the highest comic book honours.

About the illustrator

Victor Rivas was born and raised in Vigo, Spain, and he now lives outside of Barcelona. Rivas has been a freelance illustrator since 1987, working on books for children and teens, as well as magazines, posters, game animation, and comics. When he's not working, Rivas enjoys reading comics, watching cartoons and films, and playing strategy games. Most importantly, he spends as much time as possible with his daughter, Marta.

Glossary

cottage small house

crystal ball clear ball made of crystal that is used to see the future

foolish stupid or unwise

latch lock or handle for a door

palace large, grand home for a ruler or wealthy person

riding hood cloak with a hood attached that a woman wears while riding a horse

soul spiritual part of people

tender soft

wildflowers pretty flowers that grow in the wild

The history of Red Riding Hood

Many scholars believe the story of **Red Riding Hood** began as a folktale hundreds of years ago. These stories were passed down orally from generation to generation. In 1697, French author Charles Perrault wrote down the earliest known version of the story for his book *Tales of Mother Goose*. Perrault's tale, known as "Le Petit Chaperon Rouge", was different from many modern versions. In his tale, Red Riding Hood is eaten by the wolf and does not escape. Perrault knew this tragic ending would scare his readers. He wanted his story to teach a moral, or a lesson in right and wrong. In fact, at the end of the story the author left a message for his reader, stating, "Children . . . should never talk to strangers, for if they should do so, they may well provide dinner for a wolf".

Perrault's tale was popular during its time, but today's best-known version came many years later. In 1812, Jacob and Wilhelm Grimm published their book of collected stories called *Children's and Household Tales*. It included several of today's most famous fairy tales, such as "Cinderella", "Snow White", and "Rapunzel". The book also included the story of **Red Riding Hood**, which they called "Little Red Cap". Although similar to Perrault's version, "Little Red Cap" was intended to be read by children.

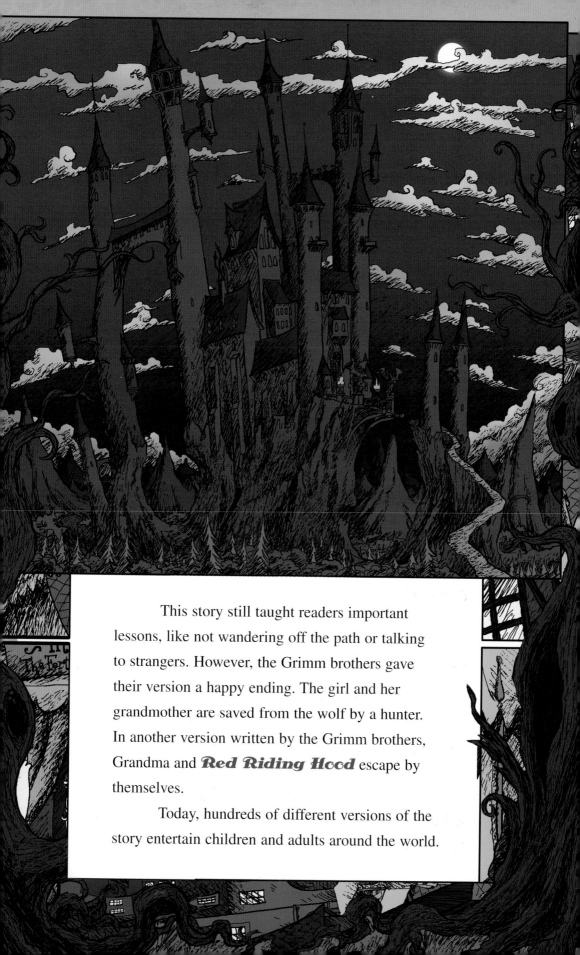

This story still taught readers important lessons, like not wandering off the path or talking to strangers. However, the Grimm brothers gave their version a happy ending. The girl and her grandmother are saved from the wolf by a hunter. In another version written by the Grimm brothers, Grandma and **Red Riding Hood** escape by themselves.

Today, hundreds of different versions of the story entertain children and adults around the world.

Discussion questions

1. Why do you think Ruby trusted the wolf? What could she have done differently to keep herself safe?

2. At the end of the story, Ruby has to harm the wolf in order to save herself. Do you think this decision was okay? Why or why not?

3. Fairy tales are often told over and over again. Have you heard the Little Red Riding Hood fairy tale before? How is this version of the story different from other versions you've heard, seen, or read?

Writing prompts

1. Fairy tales are fantasy stories, often about wizards, goblins, giants, and fairies. Many fairy tales have a happy ending. Write your own fairy tale. Then, read it to a friend or family member.

2. In this book, Ruby has a couple of good luck charms, including her red riding hood and a four-leaf clover. Do you have any good luck charms? Write about the object and why it's lucky.

3. Imagine you were being chased through a forest by the big, bad wolf. What would you do? Write a story about how you would get away and survive.

Other books in the series

Beauty and the Beast	978 1 406 24317 8
Jack and the Beanstalk	978 1 406 24319 2
Sleeping Beauty	978 1 406 24771 8

More fairy tales to enjoy

The book may be over, but the adventure is just beginning. There are many other exciting and fantastical tales for you to discover:

Grimm's Fairy Tales (Usborne Illustrated), Ruth Brocklehurst
  (Usborne, 2010)

Hans Christian Andersen's Fairy Tales (Usborne Illustrated),
  (Usborne, 2011)